HARALD SALFELLNER

BEST CZECH
RECIPES

D0914792

VITALIS
2000

© 2000 Vitalis, Prague
U Lužického semináře 19
CZ-118 00 Praha
e-mail: Vitalis@telecom.cz

The photographs in the book were processed
by the visual design editors at Vitalis,
under the guidance of the author
and with the collaboration
of the photographer Michal Pavlík.
Type-setting: Cadis, Praha
Vytiskla Severografie Most
ISBN 3-934774-19-9
ISBN 80-7253-006-2

nde co ſpodají · Lepſi kuchyně než apatika

VITALIS

Contents

Introduction 7

Bread and Pastry 9

Soups, Starters and "a little bite to go with your beer" 12

Dumplings (Knedlíky) .20

Fruit, Vegetables and Pulses 26

All About Pork 34

Beef, Veal and Other Meat Dishes 41

Poultry 52

Game 56

Fish 60

Assorted Desserts 65

Introduction

For many people, Old Bohemia, with its capital city Prague -
"Golden Prague" and the peaceful countryside of Moravia arou-
se nostalgic memories of the good old times. And just as in the
days of the Emperor, people flock to the Czech Republic today
to titillate their taste buds with the excellent local specialities,
ranging from the fine delicacies of the international spa centres
of Karlovy Vary (Carlsbad), Mariánské Lázně (Marienbad) or
Františkovy Lázně, to the ingenious single pot rustic concoc-
tions renowned in the Krkonoše (Giant Mountains) and the
Šumava.

Bohemian cuisine is influenced by two major culinary the-
mes: the German-Czech culinary tradition, with its strong re-
gional variations, dominating naturally in those parts of the
land which were inhabited mostly by Germans – and Czech-
Slavonic cooking and eating customs, which are entirely differ-
ent from the cuisine of other Slavic countries such as Russia and
Poland. A glance at the history of this land is enough to show
how many other influences were added to these important ori-
ginal sources. King Charles IV brought, among other things,
wine grapes from Burgundy, Josef Groll introduced Pilsen beer
from Bavaria, and the Tyroleans living in Volary brought, not

Tyrolean dumplings, but a little something of their Alpine eating habits to South Bohemia. The 20th century saw many additions from Slovak cuisine, and subordination to the Soviet Empire did not fail to leave its traces. The diversity of its origins justifies Czech cuisine incorporation into European cultural heritage, nourished as it has been from time immemorial by both national identities and foreign influences.

This little book gathers together the best recipes from both former times and the present day. The recipes are presented in such a way that they can be easily prepared in the average modern kitchen. We wish you successful cooking and "bon appetit", or as we say here: "Dobrou chuť!"

Harald Salfellner

The recipes – if not stated otherwise – serve 4 persons.

Lomnice Cookies (Lomnické suchary)

$^1/_4$ l milk
25 g yeast
a little sugar.
500 g flour

150 g butter
3 egg yolks
pinch of salt
grated lemon rind

Heat the milk (do not scald).
Dissolve the yeast in the milk with

Add the flour, butter and egg yolks
and work the mixture into a dough.
Mix the salt, lemon rind, nutmeg
and fennel into the dough.

Leave the dough to rise for 30 minutes, then roll out flat in two pieces. Place on a greased baking tray and leave to rise another 20 minutes. Bake at 200° for about 30 minutes. The following day, cut into slices about a finger thick and leave to dry out at 120°. While still warm, wrap in the vanilla sugar wrappings.

$^1/_2$ grated nutmeg
a knife-tip of fennel
powder
4 vanilla sugar wrappings

Apple Charlotte

10 dried bread rolls	Cut the rolls into thin slices.
1/2 l milk	Mix the milk thoroughly with the
3 eggs	eggs and sugar and
100 g sugar	leave the bread slices to soak in the mixture.
750 g apples	Peel and core apples, cut into thin slices.
50 g raisins	Mix with raisins and almond slices.
50 g almond slices	Place alternate layers of the softened rolls and apple mix into a well reased baking tin.
50 g balls of butter	Put the butter balls on the top layer of bread. Place the baking tin in a pre-heated oven at 200° and bake for 30 minutes.
2 egg whites	Mix the egg whites with the sugar and
30 g sugar	whisk into a thick mixture. Spread the pudding with the egg mixture and return to oven for 10 minutes. The top should brown slightly.

Apple Charlotte

Prague Ham (Pražská šunka) in Bread Pastry

80 g yeast 1 teaspoonful sugar 1 table spoon salt	Place the yeast in a small bowl and mix with the sugar and salt until the yeast is liquid.
500 g rye flour 250 g wheat flour 50 g corn sprouts	Mix the rye and wheat flour with the corn sprouts in a large bowl. It is best to use a fork for this, as it makes sifting unnecessary.
600 ml water	Pour the water and dissolved yeast into the bowl and mix the dough. Cover the dough and leave to rise.
1 kg ham (soaked overnight in water)	Cook the ham (soaked overnight) on low heat in a covered pan for about 1 hour. Remove skin, and leave ham to cool. Sprinkle a pastry board with flour and roll out the bread dough to a thickness of about 1 cm.
2-3 eggs	Whisk the eggs and spread half onto the dough. Place the ham on the dough and carefully wrap it in the dough. Smooth out the edges.
75 g butter	Spread the butter on a large baking tray and place on it the filled loaf. Spread on the remaining egg and pierce several times with a fork. Bake at 225° for about 2 1/2 hours

Prague Ham in Bread Pastry

Tripe Soup (Dršťková polévka)

250 g tripe	wash tripe thoroughly, steam, strain the water and
salt	bring to a boil in fresh water with the finely chopped soup vegetables.
1 onion	
soup vegetables	
1 garlic clove	
marjoram	
ginger	Add the spices, and
2 grains of pepper	leave to simmer on low heat for about 2 hours.
30 g butter	Melt the butter and
40 g flour	mix in the flour with an egg-whisk. Gradually dilute with the stock. Simmer for 10 minutes, so that the soup does not taste of flour.
100 g smoked meat	Finely chop the tripe and add it to the soup together with the diced smoked meat. Simmer for a while.
chopped parsley	Serve with parsley.

Tripe Soup (bottom), Potato Soup (centre), Cabbage Soup (top)

Cabbage Soup (Zelňačka)

40 g bacon 20 g butter 1 onion 2 garlic cloves	Dice the bacon, then heat it in the butter in a large saucepan. Chop the onion and garlic very finely and sauté until they reach a glassy consistency.
2 teaspoons sweet paprika 250 g sauerkraut salt $1/2$ teaspoons caraway seeds	Mix in the paprika. Add the sauerkraut, season with the salt and caraway seeds.
$3/4$ l meat stock	Add the meat stock and bring to a boil.
50 g butter 50 g flour $3/4$ l meat stock	In a pot, brown the butter and the flour and slowly add the meat stock. Mix the browned butters flour mixture into the soup and simmer for about 15 minutes on medium heat.
2 potatoes	Peel and chop the potatoes. Add to the soup and boil for another 15 minutes.
200 g whipped cream	Finally, add the whipped cream. You can further spice up your soup with
200 g frankfurters or salami	chopped frankfurters or salami to taste.

Garlic Soup (Česnečka)

150 g white bread	Chop the bread into small pieces and place in a warmed soup bowl.
4 garlic cloves	Finely chop the garlic and mix with the salt.
pinch of salt	Combine the garlic mixture with the bread.
1,25 l water	Bring the water to a boil and pour into the soup bowl.
40 g butter	Add the butter, and sprinkle chopped parsley over the top. Mix and serve immediately.

Beer Soup (Pivní polévka)

0,5 l beer	Pour the beer and water into a sauce-pan.
0,5 l water	
100 g dark bread, chopped into small pieces	Add the bread and bring to a boil, stirring continuously.
pinch of salt	Add the salt, mace, raisins, almonds and butter.
50 g butter	
pinch of mace	
50 g raisins	
30 g chopped almonds	Season and serve immediately.

Pickled Herrings Prague-style

Serves 8

8 herrings	Leave herring to soak for two or three days in a sufficient amount of water
a little milk	with a little milk.
	Change the liquid frequently. Then dry the herrings thoroughly, skin and bone. Remove the heads and tails and
4 table spoons of oil	fry in the oil.
1 bay leaf	
10 grains of pepper	Place in a china dish along with the bay leaf, pepper and onion.
chopped onion	Sieve the herring roe and mix with
8 table spoons of sweet cream	the cream to make a sauce.
oil and vinegar	Pour the sauce over the herrings and leave to stand, covered, for 6 days. Appropriate side dishes are potato salad, gherkins, capers and baby onions.

PRAKTICKÁ
KUCHAŘKA
OD M. RETIKOVÉ.

CENA 70 HAL.

DRUHÉ DOPLNĚNÉ VYDÁNÍ.

Bohemian Bread Dumplings
(Houskové knedlíky)

15 g yeast 1 teaspoonful sugar 1 pinch of salt 400 g flour	Mix the yeast and sugar well until the yeast is liquid. Pour the flour into a bowl. Add the liquid yeast,
3 eggs 1/8 l milk	eggs, and milk, and knead into a dough. Leave to rise for an hour.
1 bread roll from the day before 40 g butter	Cut the bread roll into small pieces, sauté lightly in the butter and when cooled, work into the dough. On a floured pastry board, work the dough into two oblong loaves. Cover with a tea cloth and leave to rise for another 15 minutes.
4 l salted water	In a large saucepan, bring the water to boil and place one of the loaves in it. When the water begins to boil again, add the second loaf. Bring to boil again, then turn the heat down as low as possible and leave the dumplings to cook for 15 minutes. Half way through the cooking, turn the dumplings over. Cut into slices and serve.

Bohemian Potato, Bread and Flour Dumplings

Raised Dumplings (Kynuté knedlíky)

15 g yeast	Dissolve yeast in lukewarm milk, add sugar and let the yeast rise.
a little sugar	
500 g flour	Mix with the flour.
1 egg	Add the egg and salt and mix thoroughly. Leave to rise for an hour and then form into dumplings on a floured pastry board. Cover with a tea cloth and leave again to rise. Boil the dumplings for 15 minutes in a covered saucepan, then remove the lid and leave dumplings to cook for another few minutes. Strain well, cut into slices and pour on melted butter.
a pinch of salt	

Potato Dumplings (Bramborové knedlíky)

500 g floury potatoes	Boil potatoes in their skins, peel while still hot and leave to cool. Transfer potatoes to a pastry board, make a hole in the centre.
1 egg 2 pinches of salt 80 g flour 80 g semolina	Add the egg, salt, flour and semolina and mix into a hard firm dough.
4 l salted water	Make 5 oblong dumplings out of the mixture, place them all together in the salted water and let simmer on medium heat for 15 minutes. After 8 minutes, turn over carefully. When ready, cut into slices and serve.

Fruit Dumplings (Ovocné knedlíky)

15 g yeast	Mix the yeast and the sugar thoroughly
40 g sugar	
1 pinch of salt	until the yeast is liquid.
250 g flour	Sieve the flour into a bowl. Add the liquid yeast,
1 egg,	egg and
¼ l milk	
1 packet	
of vanilla sugar	milk and vanilla sugar and work into a dough. Leave to rise for 30 minutes, then roll the dough into a thin square and cut into 20 small squares.
20 plums or apricots	Wash fruit and remove stones. If the fruit is not yet ripe enough, you can insert a sugar cube in place of the stone. Place the fruit on the pieces of dough and with wet hands wrap the fruit in the dough.
3 litres salted water	Bring the water to the boil, divide dumplings into 4 portions and cook each portion separately for 20 minutes on medium heat. When cooked, remove, pierce several times with a fork and store in a warm place until all dumplings are ready.
200 g butter	Finally, melt the butter, pour over the dumplings just before serving and sprinkle dumplings with
150 g icing sugar	icing sugar and grated tvaroh.
a 400 g grated hard tvaroh (Czech cream cheese)	

Fruit Dumplings

Barley with Mushrooms (Kuba)

40 g dried mushrooms $1/2$ l water	Wash mushrooms in a sieve and leave to soak, covered, for 20 minutes.
300 g barley 40 g melted butter $1/2$ l meat stock pinch of salt	Brown the barley in the butter, pour on the meat stock, season with salt and add the mushrooms with the water used for soaking. Stew, covered, for 50 minutes on medium heat, stirring occasionally.
2 onions 4 garlic cloves	Peel the onions and garlic, chop finely, sauté in butter until consistency is glassy
40 g melted butter $1/8$ l water 1 teaspoon caraway seeds 1 teaspoon marjoram	and add to the barley. Add the water and seasoning. Place the mixture in a well greased baking tin, bake uncovered for 15 minutes at 200° in a pre-heated oven and serve immediately.

Barley with Mushrooms (Kuba)

Sauerkraut (Kyselé zelí)

1 onion	Chop onion into small pieces and
50 g pork fat	brown in the pork fat.
500 g sauerkraut	Add the sauerkraut,
pinch of salt	season with salt and caraway seeds.
1 teaspoon caraway	
seeds	Pour on a little water and boil the sauer-
	kraut until soft. After about half an hour,
1 raw potato	add the raw potato to the sauerkraut
	and cook on medium heat for another
	15 minutes.

Pancakes with Spinach

4 egg yolks	Using an egg whisk, mix the egg yolks,
1 tablespoon flour	flour, milk, water, salt and mace into
1 tablespoon milk	a light dough.
1 tablespoon water	
1 pinch of salt	
1 pinch of mace	
250 g spinach (fresh)	Wash the spinach, chop finely and mix
	in with the dough.
4 egg whites	Whisk the egg whites into a thick snow
	and mix into the dough.
1 tablespoon butter	Melt the butter in a frying pan and fry
	4 pancakes, 2 minutes for each side.
	Transfer to a plate and serve with salad.

Potato Pancakes (Bramboráky)

1 kg potatoes	Wash, peel and grate potatoes.
1/8 l milk	Warm the milk, and pour over the potatoes.
120 g flour	Mix in the flour and eggs.
3 eggs	
100 g bacon	Chop the bacon, dripping and garlic into
40 g drippings	small pieces and crush with the salt, pepper
4 garlic cloves	and marjoram.
salt, pepper	
3 teaspoons	
marjoram	Mix in with the potato mixture and fry the pancakes one by one in oil, allowing 4-5 minutes for each side.
100 ml oil	The pancakes should be served immediately when ready.

Potato Pancake

Sour Lentils (Čočka na kyselo)

300 g lentils	Wash the lentils under running water and cover with cold water.
2 bay leaves	Add the bay leaves, and cook for 25 minutes on medium/high heat, stirring occasionally.
30 g butter	
30 g flour	Prepare a browning from the butter, flour and
1/4 l meat stock	stock.
100 g cream	Pour on the cream, season with
1/2 teaspoons salt	salt and boil gently on medium/high heat for about 10 minutes, stirring occasionally, taking care not to burn the browning. Pour the lentils, with the water in which they boiled, into the sauce.
1 onion	Peel and dice the onion,
50 g butter	fry in butter until golden, add the lentils, season with the
1 tablespoon vinegar	vinegar and boil for another 5 minutes.
4 large gherkins	Finely chop the gherkins and mix into the lentils prior to serving.

Stuffed Kohlrabi (Plněné kedlubny)

4 kohlrabi	Peel the kohlrabi and boil for 30 minutes
2 litres salted water	in the salted water. Leave kohlrabi to cool in the water. Stuffing:
1 small onion	Peel the onion and
1 garlic clove	garlic, chop finely and sauté in
60 g butter	butter until consistency is glassy.
100 g champignons	Wash the mushrooms, cut into thin slices and fry for a short while with the onion and garlic.
150 g minced beef	Add the minced beef and fry for a short while. Leave the mixture to cool, mix in
1 egg	the egg
salt	and salt
mace	and mace. When the cabbages have cooled, carefully scrape out the flesh and fill with the meat and mushroom stuffing.
1 tablespoon butter	Grease a fireproof baking dish with butter, place the stuffed cabbages into it, chop the scraped out flesh into pieces and put in between the cabbages. Pour on 300 ml of the cabbage stock, cover, and bake at 180° in a pre-heated oven. Store the cabbages in a warm place.
2 tablespoon flour	Mix the flour and
200 g whipped cream	cream, pour into the sauce,
salt	season with salt and
mace	mace, bring the to boil and simmer for 10 minutes on medium heat. Stir the sauce and serve with the cabbages.

Potato Gnocchi (Škubánky)

1 kg potatoes	Peel the potatoes, cut into squares and boil in salted water until soft. Strain the potatoes, but keep the water. Mash the potatoes and
150 g flour	mix with the flour. Pour on ⅛ l of the potato water. Stew the mixture, covered, on minimum heat. After about 10 minutes, pour off the extra water and stir the mashed potatoes again thoroughly.
50 g fat	Heat the fat, and use a damp tablespoon to put the gnocchi in the fat. (This makes it easier.)
1 tablespoon chopped onion sugar ground poppy seed	Fry the onion for sprinkling on top, or mix sugar with poppy seeds.

Potato Gnocchi

Moravian Sparrow (Moravský vrabec)

400 g side of pork	Wash and dry the meat, and make several cuts in the skin with a sharp knife.
400 g shoulder of pork	Carve both pieces of meat into 4 equal portions.
4 garlic cloves	Peel and crush the garlic and mix with
1 teaspoon salt	the salt
1 teaspoon caraway	and caraway seeds. Spread this paste evenly on the pieces of meat.
4 large onions	Peel the onions, dice and fry in the
60 g pork fat	pork fat. Place the meat skin down on the onion and pour the
150 ml hot water	hot water on top. Roast the meat for about 1 1/2 hour. Serve with the juice and onion.

Moravian Sparrow

Spicy Roast Pork

1-1,5 kg pork leg	Wash the meat, dry thoroughly, and slice the skin into ovals with a sharp knife.
4 garlic cloves 1 teaspoon salt a little pepper	Peel and crush the garlic, mix with the salt and pepper
1 teaspoon caraway	and caraway seeds. Spread this mixture on the meat.
4 bay leaves	Quarter the bay leaves and insert into the cuts in the skin, together with the
8 grains new spice 8 grains black pepper 4 juniper berries.	spice, peppers and juniper berries.
5 spoonfuls of oil	Briefly roast the leg in the oil, with the skin underneath, and pour on the
1/4 l hot water	hot water. Place the covered roasting dish in a pre-heated oven at 200° and roast for 2 or 2 1/2 hours. Turn the meat after an hour. Then leave in a warm place and strain the juice.
3 tablespoons flour 1/4 l water	Mix in the flour, add the water and simmer on low heat for 15 minutes. Carve the meat into slices, and serve the sauce separately.

Spicy Pork with Dumplings and sauerkraut

Bohemian Pork Goulash

750 g shoulder of pork	Chop into small pieces.
5 tablespoons oil	Heat the oil in a wide casserole dish and fry the meat quickly in it.
1 pepper	
4 tomatoes	
3 large onions	Finely chop the pepper, tomatoes, onions and
2 garlic cloves	garlic, briefly fry with the meat. Season with
pinch of salt	
1/2 teaspoons paprika	
1/2 teaspoons caraway	salt and spices
1/4 l vegetable stock	and pour on the vegetable stock. Cook the goulash for about 45 minutes, until the meat is soft. Remove the dish from the heat and mix
100 g sour cream	the cream into the goulash.

Piquant Meat and Vegetable Cakes

2 carrots	
1/8 celery	
1 turnip	
1 onion	Wash, peel and finely chop the vegetables.
1/8 head of Savoy cabbage	
	Simmer vegetables,
1 l water	strain and press.
1 bread roll	Soak the bread roll in the
1/8 l milk	milk, squeeze dry and add to the vegetables.
300 g mincemeat	Add the mincemeat, garlic, egg and
4 crushed garlic cloves	
1 egg	
100 g breadcrumbs	breadcrumbs, mix together thoroughly. Season the meat-vegetable dough with
salt, pepper	salt and pepper and
1 teaspoon marjoram	marjoram. With wet hands, form 8 flat cakes about 1 cm thick, and
1/8 l oil	fry heavily on both sides for about 3 minutes. Reduce the heat to a minimum, cover the pan with a lid, and bake for another 5 minutes on both sides. Remove pan from heat and let the cakes cook for another 5 minutes.

Brno Cutlet (Brněnský řízek)

4 large pork cutlets	Wash the cutlets, dry well, cut into thin slices and rub both sides with
4 pinches salt	salt.
150 g boiled ham	Cut the ham into small pieces and
40 g butter	fry in the butter.
3 eggs	Whisk eggs and add to the frying pan.
6 tablespoons peas (frozen)	Lastly, add the peas and stew for about 2 minutes. Spread this mixture on the meat slices. Remove from pan and join with toothpicks.
2 tablespoons flour	Coat the cutlets with the flour.
2 eggs	Whisk the eggs
2 tablespoons milk	with the milk. Dip the meat in this mixture on both sides,
4 tablespoons breadcrumbs	then coat in breadcrumbs.
1/8 l oil	Heat the oil in a large pan, fry the cutlets on both sides, then finish for 45 minutes on low heat.

Veal Cutlets in Cream
(Telecí řízky na smetaně)

4 veal cutlets · Wash the cutlets, dry well, and
4 pinches salt · season with salt.
4 tablespoons flour · Coat the cutlets in the flour.
100 g melted butter · Fry in butter for about 5 minutes on
each side. Cover pan, and leave cutlets
to stew on low heat for 45 minutes.
Make a browning for the sauce from the

30 g butter
30 g flour
1/8 l white wine
a 1/8 l water · butter, flour, wine and water. Add
200 g whipped cream · the cream and simmer for 15 minutes,
stirring constantly.

1 sprig of parsley · Finely chop the parsley,
4 anchovies · anchovies and
4 teaspoons capers · capers and add to the sauce. Leave the
cutlets to cook in the sauce for another
15 minutes and serve with the sauce.

41

Roast Pork in Sour Sauce
(Pečeně s kyselou omáčkou)

Serves 6

2 large onions	
2 carrots	
1 parsnip	Clean and slice the vegetables.
1/4 celery	
1 sprig of levisticum	
2 bay leaves	
8 grains of black pepper	
and 8 of new spice	
8 juniper berries	Place in a large bowl with the seasoning and spices.
2 teaspoons of thyme	
1200 g roasting beef	Wash and dry the beef, and place in the vegetable mixture.
	Pour on the
1/4 l red wine	red wine and oil until the meat is
1/4 l oil	completely submerged. Cover bowl and leave in a cool place. The meat must stand in the liquid for at least a day; the taste will be more tender if you leave it in for 3-4 days. In the latter case you should turn the joint at least once a day.
	Remove meat from liquid, let it drain

42

1 teaspoon salt
3 tablespoons oil

thoroughly and rub with salt. Quickly fry in the oil. Strain off the liquid and briefly fry the vegetables with the meat. Pour on about 200 ml of the liquid, and roast in a covered casserole dish for about 3 hours in a preheated oven at 190°. The meat should be turned regularly and topped up with the liquid. Add the remaining liquid gradually to the meat. When ready, keep the meat warm, remove the bay leaves, juniper berries and new spice from the sauce and stir. Lastly, mix in the

250 g whipped cream

cream and bring the sauce to a boil once more. Carve the meat into slices, and serve the sauce separately.

Carlsbad Roll

1,5 kg veal breast prepared for cooking	Wash and dry the meat, and make a deep incision in the middle. Separate the slices of meat and rub with
4 pinches salt 150 g boiled ham 150 g raw ham 2 gherkins	the salt. Lay the ham on top,
	finely chop the gherkins and sprinkle over the meat.
4 eggs	Whisk the eggs with the
2 pinches salt	salt and
2 tablespoons milk	milk
2 teaspoons butter	and fry in butter to make scrambled eggs. Lay the scrambled eggs on the meat. Roll the meat, and close firmly with meat skewers or butcher's thread. In a baking tin, fry the meat on all sides in
60 g butter	the butter. Cover the tin, place in a pre-heated oven at 200° and roast meat for about 2 1/2 hours. Turn the meat occasionally, add water if necessary. Keep the joint warm, and mix
1 tablespoon butter	the butter into the dripping.
1 tablespoon flour	Add the flour
1/8 l meat stock	and dilute with the meat stock. Leave the sauce to simmer for 15 minutes on low heat. Carve the meat into slices and serve in the sauce.

Carlsbad Roll

Brno Lamb Ribs in Wine Sauce

500 g lamb ribs	Divide the ribs into 4 pieces, slice off the fat and part of the skin. Tenderize the meat and
1 garlic clove	rub thoroughly with the garlic.
salt	Season with salt.
50 g fat	Heat the fat in a frying pan, and
1 chopped onion	fry the onion and vegetables in it.
200 g soup vegetables	After about 3 minutes, add the meat.
125 g boiled ham	Dice the ham and sprinkle over the lamb ribs.
1/4 l white wine	Pour on the wine and stew for about 40 minutes until soft. Remove meat from pan and transfer to a pre-heated bowl. Strain the sauce and pour over the meat.

Brno Lamb Ribs in Wine Sauce

Fillet of Beef (Svíčková pečeně)

650 g fillet of beef	Wash, remove skin and tendons.
50 g bacon	Cut bacon into noodles and insert it into the beef.
salt and pepper	Season lightly.
3 tablespoons oil	Heat oil in a casserole dish until hot and fry the meat on all sides.
soup vegetables	Finely chop the vegetables and
1 onion	onion and add to the meat
1 bay leaf	
black pepper	
thyme	
10 chopped capers	
grated lemon rind	with the spices. Fry for a short while.
1 tablespoon vinegar	
2 tablespoons Madeira	Pour on the vinegar and Madeira and
1/8 l stock	stock, cover the pan, and stew approx. 45 minutes until soft. Strain the juices and thicken
1 tablespoon flour	with the flour
1/8 l sour cream	and sour cream. Pour the sauce over the meat and serve.

Fillet of Beef

Sirloin (Roštěná)

4 slices of sirloin	Wash sirloin in running water, dry thoroughly. Make several cuts in the fat on the edge of the slices, and
salt, pepper, ground caraway seed 4 crushed garlic cloves	apply the seasoning and garlic to the fat.
	Wrap the meat in
4 tablespoons flour	the flour and fry quickly in butter in a cast-iron pan
80 g melted butter	(about 5 minutes for each side).
1/8 l meat stock	Pour on the stock, cover, and stew on low heat for approx. one hour. Keep the meat warm,
200 g sour cream	add the cream to the dripping. Serve the meat slices in the sauce.

Sirloin

Roast Goose (Pečená husa)

Serves 8

1 gutted goose (approx. 4 kg)	Wash thoroughly under running water, dry well and
salt and pepper	rub with salt and pepper.
1 kg cooking apples	Peel and core the apples, and add to the gutted goose
1 sprig of thyme or wormwood	with the thyme. Close the neck and breast openings with needles or cocktoothpicks, place the goose in a roasting tin, about
1/4 l hot water	and pour on the hot water. Cover, place in a pre-heated oven at 210° and cook for approx. 4 hours. Turn regularly and occasionally top up with dripping. Uncover for the last half-hour, and roast the goose until golden. Remove needles and serve with the dripping.

Roast Goose

Stewed Duck in Mushroom Sauce

1 duck (approx. 2.5 kg)	Split the duck into 4 portions, wash thoroughly in running water and dry well.
1 teaspoon salt	Rub the portions with salt
2 teaspoon thyme	
80 g melted butter	and thyme, melt the butter in a casserole dish and fry on all sides.
250 ml meat stock	Pour on the stock,
2 bay leaves	
4 juniper berries	add the seasoning
6 grains each of new spice and black pepper	and spices. Cover and leave to stew for approx. 2 hours. For the sauce,
200 g fresh mushrooms	wash and slice the mushrooms,
1 tablespoon butter	and fry in the butter.
2 tablespoon flour	Whisk the flour
150 ml cream	and the cream together, mix into the dripping and simmer briefly. Leave to simmer for 10 minutes on medium heat, then remove from heat.
2 egg yolks	Whisk the yolks
50 ml cream	with the cream and mix into the sauce. Add the mushrooms and
1 tablespoon lemon juice	season with the lemon juice. Serve the duck and sauce separately.

Stewed Duck in Mushroom Sauce

Saddle of Venison Bohemian-style

Serves 8

1 saddle of venison	Remove skin and pierce venison with a needle.
150 g bacon	Cut the bacon into strips and insert them into the venison.
salt, pepper	Rub with salt and pepper
juniper berries	and pressed juniper berries.
120 g fat	Heat the fat in a roasting dish and place the venison in the dish, bacon side down.
1 onion	Cut the onion into rings, and place on the meat
thin lemon slices	with the lemon slices. Pour the hot fat over
vinegar	the meat and sprinkle a little vinegar on top. Pre-heat the oven to 200° and cook the venison for 1 1/2 to 2 1/2 hours, according to size, until tender.
1/8 l sour cream	Mix the sour cream with water, and from time to time pour onto the meat. Half way though the cooking time, turn the meat and roast the other side until crisp and golden. As soon as the meat is cooked through, remove from oven, slice with a carving knife and keep warm. Let the dripping thicken slightly,
20 g flour	sprinkle on the flour, simmer, then sieve. Serve sauce separately.

Saddle of Venison Bohemian-style

Wild Duck with Onion

1 gutted wild duck (approx. 2 kg)	Wash thoroughly in running water, dry and season with
salt and pepper	salt and pepper on the inside and outside.
3-4 onions	Peel the onions, chop into squares and place inside the gutted duck
1 bay leaf	with the bay leaf and
4 juniper berries	juniper berries. Sew the duck up with butcher's thread and tie the wings and legs firmly to the body.
300 g bacon	Cut the bacon into thin slices and lay on the duck.
60 g melted butter	Heat the butter in a roasting dish and place the duck in the dish. Cover the dish, place in an oven pre-heated to 200° and roast the duck for 1 1/2 hours. Occasionally pour the juice over the top. Finally, remove the bacon, uncover the dish and let the duck roast until golden.
2 tablespoons flour	For the sauce, boil the juices, stir and sprinkle in the flour,
1/4 l white wine	slowly add the wine
1/4 l meat stock	and the stock. Let the sauce simmer for 10 minutes on medium heat, remove the bay leaves and juniper berries and serve the sauce with the duck portions.

Rabbit (králík) in Cream Sauce

1 gutted rabbit	Remove fine membranes, wash, cut into 4 portions and smear with
1 teaspoon salt	salt. Place the portions in a casserole dish and
50 g melted butter	fry rapidly in butter on all sides. Reduce heat to a minimum,
2 large onion	peel the onions, cut into squares and add to the meat.
2 carrots	
1/8 celery	Wash the vegetables, peel, and cut into thin slices.
1/2 parsnip	Sauté for approx. 10 minutes with the meat.
1 teaspoon paprika (sweet)	Mix in the paprika and pour on the stock gradually.
1/4 l meat stock	Cover the pan and let the rabbit stew for approx. 2 1/2 hours. Finally, lay the meat aside in a warm place,
200 g whipped cream	add the cream to the sauce, bring to a boil and stir. Place the rabbit portions in the sauce and serve.

Carp (kapr) with Anchovies

1 carp (approx. 2 kg)	Fillet the carp, remove the scales, wash thoroughly and dry.
50 ml lemon juice	Sprinkle on the lemon and lay aside for 1/2 hour.
1 onion,	
1 carrot	Peel the vegetables,
1/8 celery	cut into small pieces and sauté in the
60 g butter	butter in a casserole dish.
1/8 l wine	Add the wine.
4 potatoes	Boil the potatoes in their skins, peel, and fill the carp with them. Place the carp on the vegetables, spine up,
8 anchovies	lay the anchovies on top
2 tablespoons breadcrumbs	and sprinkle with the breadcrumbs.
50 g knobs of butter	Place the butter knobs on the carp, place the carp in a covered roasting dish, and roast in a pre-heated oven at 180°, occasionally dousing in the juice. Serve the carp with the vegetables and potatoes.

Carp with Anchovies

Carp in Paprika Sauce

1 carp (approx. 2 kg)	Remove scales, gut, wash, slice into portions and bone. Cut off the gills and fins and throw away. Put the fish slices and bones into the wine
2-3 onions, 1 carrot 1/2 leek	with the vegetables
4 grains new spice 2 bay leaves 1/4 l white wine	spice and bay leaves and boil for approx. 1 1/2 hours on medium heat. Strain off the stock. Sprinkle the fish portions with
juice of one lemon	the lemon juice and leave for 30 minutes.
1 onion 60 g butter 1/2 teaspoonful of paprika (sweet)	Peel the onion, cut into small pieces and brown in butter. Add the paprika, allow a foam to form, then slowly add the fish stock.
1 teaspoon salt	Salt the fish slices and stew in the sauce for 15 minutes.
2 tablespoons flour 200 g cream	Whisk the flour with the cream, keep the fish warm and mix the cream into the stock.

Bring to a boil, and simmer for 10 minutes, stirring occasionally. Put the fish helpings on a warmed plate, pour sauce on top and serve.

Roast Pike (Pečená štika)

1 kg pike	Wash the fish and remove skin.
salt	Smear with salt,
juice of $^1/_2$ lemon	sprinkle inside and outside with lemon juice, and
150 g butter	sauté in the butter. Roast in oven at 190°, dousing periodically with the butter.
lemon slices	Serve the carp garnished with lemon slices
chopped parsley	and chopped parsley.

Tench (lín) Bohemian-style

1 tench (approx. 1 kg)	Prepare the fish for cooking. At the killing, preserve the blood. Before scraping off the scales, soak for about a minute in boiling water. Portion the fish,
salt	sprinkle with salt and leave for an hour.
100 g butter	Then heat the butter in a saucepan and sauté the fish slices.
2 onion cloves	Cut the onions in half and spike with cloves. Add to the fish with the
grated rind of ¹/₂ lemon	lemon rind and
200 g celery	celery. Cover the pan and stew for 15 minutes. Then turn over the fish slices and
2 tablespoons flour	sprinkle with flour.
¹/₄ l pea stock	Pour the pea stock
2 tablespoons vinegar	with the vinegar and blood onto the fish and cook for a further 5 minutes. Strain off the sauce before serving.

Griddle-Cakes (Lívance)

25 g yeast	Mix well the yeast,
70 g sugar	sugar and
1 pinch of salt	salt, until the yeast is liquid.
300 g flour	Sieve the flour into a bowl, add the liquid yeast,
3 egg	eggs and
1/2 l milk	milk and knead into a dough. Heat a cast-iron pan for 10 minutes,
bacon	and grease with bacon. Using a ladle, put the dough in the pan so that little cakes are formed, about 10 cm in diameter. Fry until golden, allowing 1-2 minutes for each side, and keep warm until all the pancakes are ready. For each separate cooking, grease the pan well with bacon. When all the pancakes are cooked,
100 g butter	melt the butter, pour onto the pancakes, place them on top of each other, and leave to stand for 10 minutes, keeping them warm. Serve on a warmed plate,
60 g icing sugar	sprinkle with icing sugar
1 level teaspoon cinnamon	and cinnamon.

Jam Patties (Povidlové taštičky)

Serves 6

300 g flour	Sieve the flour onto a pastry board.
1 egg,	Quickly work the egg,
a little salt	salt and
4 tablespoons milk	milk into a dough. Roll out the dough to a thickness of 1/2 cm, and cut into flat cakes about the size of the palm of the hand.
100 g plum jam	Flavour the jam with
1 tablespoon rum	rum,
a little cinnamon	
and sugar	cinnamon and sugar, and divide equally between the patties.
1 egg	Whisk the egg with water and paste onto the dough. Fold the edges of the patties over each other and join firmly. Put the patties in boiling water for approx. 6 minutes and boil until they float to the top. Remove with a sieve-ladle and rinse briefly in cold water. Dry and
150 g breadcrumbs	coat in breadcrumbs.
2-3 spoonfuls	
icing sugar	Sprinkle with icing sugar before serving.

Jam Patties

Ducat Cakes (Dukátové buchtičky)

25 g yeast	Mix the yeast,
50 g sugar	sugar and
1 pinch of salt	salt thoroughly, until liquid.
100 g butter	Briefly heat the butter and
1/4 l milk	pour on the milk.
500 g flour	Sieve the flour into a bowl. Add the milk, yeast and
3 egg yolks	yolks and work into a dough. Leave to rise for 1/2 hour, then roll out on a floured pastry board to about finger thickness. Cut into small circles using a small glass. Grease frying pan thoroughly, add the cakes and leave to rise for another 1/2 hour.
2 tablespoons oil	Smear with oil and bake in a pre-heated oven at 200° for 30 minutes, until golden. Turn out while hot and
2 tablespoons icing sugar	sprinkle with icing sugar. Serve cold with chocolate sauce.

Ducat Cakes

Pancakes (Palačinky)

200 g flour	Mix the flour with the
1/2 l milk,	milk,
2 eggs	eggs and
1 pinch of salt.	salt into a smooth dough, leave to expand, then
oil	cook 4-5 pancakes in heated oil. Spread with marmalade
4 tablespoons marmalade	and roll. Palačinky are also excellent with spice or filled with fruit, ice cream and whipped cream.

Sunday Bábovka

25 g yeast	Mix thoroughly the yeast,
40 g sugar	sugar and
1 pinch of salt	salt, until liquid.
500 g flour	Work the flour,
4 egg yolks	yolks,
100 g butter	butter,
1/4 l milk	milk and liquid yeast into a soft dough.
140 g raisins	Mix the raisins and
50 g chopped almonds	almonds into the dough. Grease the bábovka mould (hollow fluted dome shape) and
1 tablespoon breadcrumbs	sprinkle with breadcrumbs. Pour the dough into the mould and leave to rise for 30 minutes. Pre-heat oven to 190° and bake the bábovka for 50-60 minutes. While warm,
1 packet vanilla sugar	sprinkle with the vanilla sugar and
1 tablespoon icing sugar	icing sugar.

Scones (Vdolky)

25 g yeast	Mix the yeast,
2 teaspoons sugar	sugar
1 pinch of salt	and salt thoroughly, until liquid.
400 g flour	Sieve the flour into a bowl. Add the liquid yeast,
2 eggs	eggs,
1/4 l milk	milk and
1 packet of vanilla sugar	vanilla sugar and work into a dough. Leave to rise for 30 minutes, then divide the dough into 8 pieces. On a floured pastry board, form each piece into a small bun, and leave to rise for another 15 minutes. Then shape the buns into round cakes and fry in a large saucepan
300 ml oil	in the oil, allowing about 4 minutes for each side. Let drain for a while and
400 g plum jam	smear with the jam and
400 g cream cheese (tvaroh)	cheese. Serve immediately.

Scones

Prague Nutty Cake

4 egg yolks	Whisk the egg yolks
60 g sugar	with the sugar to make a foam. In a second bowl, whisk the
4 egg whites	egg whites and
1 pinch of salt	salt into a viscous snow, gradually add the
50 icing sugar	icing sugar until a viscous icy snow is formed. Mix this carefully into the egg yolk mixture. Add the
100 g grated biscuits	
100 g ground walnuts	biscuits and walnuts in spoonfuls and mix.
1 teaspoon baking powder	Add the baking powder. Grease and sprinkle the cake mold, place the dough in the muld and place immediately in the oven, pre.-heated to 170°. Bake for 35 minutes, leave to cool for a while, carefully loosen the edges and turn out the cake onto a grill. When completely cool, slice in half with cutting thread.
150 g butter	Whisk to butter into a foam, gradually add
100 g icing sugar	
2 egg yolks	
1 packet vanilla sugar	the icing sugar, egg yolks, vanilla sugar and
1 tablespoon rum	rum. Spread the cream on the lower half of the cake, place the other half on top and press down lightly.
150 g icing sugar	Mix the icing sugar, water and
2 tablespoons water	
2 tablespoons rum	rum into a smooth sauce and coat the surface and sides on the cake. For garnish,
200 g whipped cream	whip the cream thickly
2 tablespoons icing sugar	with the icing sugar and
1 tablespoon cocoa powder	cocoa powder, put into a squeezer and form 12 rosettes on the sauce, when it is dry. Decorate the rosettes with
12 walnut halves	the walnut halves and leave to chill for 2 hours.

Prague Nutty Cake

Christmas Cake (Vánočka)

100 g raisins	Soak the raisins in the rum
5 tablespoons of rum	and set aside.
30 g yeast	Mix the yeast,
100 g sugar	sugar and
1 pinch of salt	salt thoroughly, until liquid.
200 g butter	Heat the butter in a small pan, and pour into the
200 ml milk	milk. Mix all with
500 g flour	the flour,
3 eggs	eggs and
1 packet of vanilla sugar	vanilla sugar and work into a soft dough. Mix the soaked raisins
120 g chopped almonds	and the almonds
120 g whole almonds (peeled)	into a dough. The more you knead the dough, the lighter the cake will be. The dough must be kneaded for at least 15 minutes, then left in a warm place for an hour to rise. Divide the dough into three, roll out into pieces about 40 cm long and form into plaits.
1 egg yolk	Smear with the egg yolk and place on a greased baking tray. Leave to rise for another 30 minutes, then bake for 50 minutes in an oven pre-heated at 180°.

Bohemian Shredded Pancake

250 g flour	Mix the flour,
1/2 l milk,	milk,
3 egg yolks	egg yolks and
1 pinch of salt	salt into a thin dough. If necessary, add
2 tablespoons sugar	the sugar.
3 egg whites	Whisk the egg whites into a viscous snow and mix into the dough.
500 g sour cherries	Drain the cherries, and add to the dough with the
20 g raisins	raisins. Heat the
50 g butter	butter in a large frying pan and pour on the dough. After about 5 minutes, turn the pancake over and shred into large pieces with a fork. After another 4 minutes of cooking, put into a bowl and
2 tablespoons icing sugar	sprinkle with icing sugar. Serve hot.

Punch

Boil 500 g sugar with 100 ml water in a new casserole dish. When boiling add the strained juice from 2 lemons and 1 orange. Remove from heat immediately, before it becomes hot, and stir in 400 ml of good quality rum. Decant into bottles. It is served as a syrup, in punch glasses diluted with water. This punch is simple to prepare, but delicious and leaves no hangover.

hlad nejlepši kuchař · Nezdoma co máš ·